W9-CEW-371

3 1842 02951 3346

KIDS SAVE
THE EARTH

Save
WATER
Every Day

by Mari Schuh

amicus
high interest

Amicus High Interest is published by Amicus
P.O. Box 1329, Mankato, MN 56002
www.amicuspublishing.us

Copyright © 2014. International copyright reserved in all countries.
No part of this book may be reproduced in any form without written
permission from the publisher.

Library of Congress Cataloging-in-Publication Data
Schuh, Mari C., 1975-
  Save water every day / Mari Schuh.
     pages cm. -- (Kids save the earth)
  Includes index.
  ISBN 978-1-60753-519-5 (hardcover) -- ISBN 978-1-60753-550-8 (eBook)
  1. Water--Environmental aspects--Juvenile literature. I. Title.
  GB662.3.S346 2014
  333.91'16--dc23
                                2013010602

Photo Credits: Fedorova Alexandra/Shutterstock Images, cover; Mike
Flippo/Shutterstock Images, 2; Thinkstock, 5; Red Line Editorial, 6; Igor
Kolos/Shutterstock Images, 9; Maximus Art/Shutterstock Images, 10;
Shutterstock Images, 13, 19, 20; Evgeny Karandaev/Shutterstock Images,
14; Jim Barber/Shutterstock Images, 17; Svetlana Lukienko/Shutterstock
Images, 23

Produced for Amicus by The Peterson Publishing Company
and Red Line Editorial.

Editor Jenna Gleisner
Designer Becky Daum
Printed in the United States of America
Mankato, MN
July, 2013
PA 1938
10 9 8 7 6 5 4 3 2 1

TABLE OF CONTENTS

The Earth's Water   4

The Water Cycle   6

Keep Water Clean   8

Use Every Drop   10

Save Water at Home   12

Save Water in the Kitchen   14

Save Water Outside   16

How to Save Rainwater   18

Save Water at School   20

Get Started Today   22

Words to Know   23

Learn More   24

Index   24

THE EARTH'S WATER

The Earth has a lot of water. Most of it is in the oceans. We can't drink this water because it has salt in it. We use water from the ground, lakes, and rivers.

How the Water Cycle Works

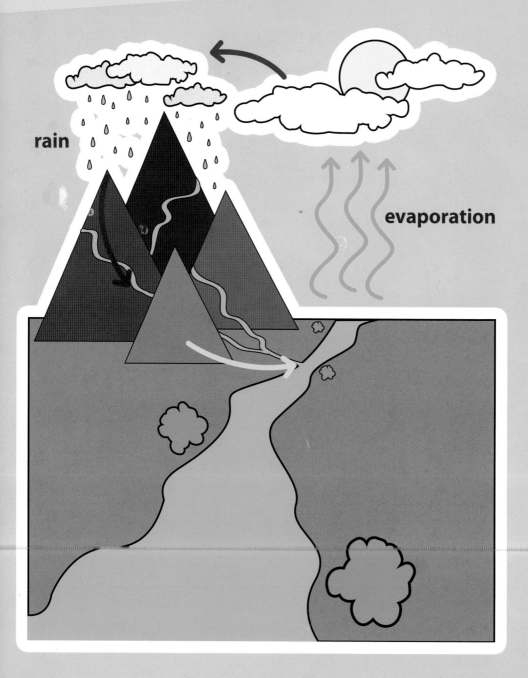

rain

evaporation

THE WATER CYCLE

Water moves around the Earth. Rain falls from clouds. It falls into lakes, rivers, and oceans. The sun **evaporates** the water. Then it rises back into the sky. Clouds form again.

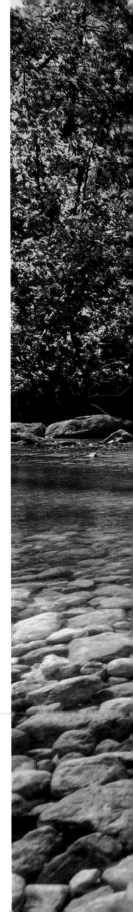

KEEP WATER CLEAN

We need clean water. Trash in rivers and lakes makes water dirty. Keep water clean. Pick up trash near rivers and lakes. An adult can help you.

USE EVERY DROP

There are more and more people on Earth. We need to share Earth's water. We can all make every drop count. Help save water at home and outside.

Let's Do It

Only turn water on halfway. Don't turn it on full blast. You will use less water.

SAVE WATER AT HOME

We can save water in many ways. Every bit helps. Start in the bathroom. Turn off the water while you brush your teeth. Only use the water you need.

Let's Do It

Take a short shower. Short showers use less water than baths. Keep it less than five minutes.

14

SAVE WATER IN THE KITCHEN

Save ice cubes when you are done with a drink. Don't throw them in the sink. Use them to water a plant.

Let's Do It

Only run the dishwasher when it is full. You won't have to run it so many times. This will save water.

SAVE WATER OUTSIDE

Is your bike dirty? Don't wash it with a hose. Hoses use lots of water. Try a new way. Use a sponge and pail. You will use much less water.

HOW TO SAVE RAINWATER

Collect the **rainwater** that runs off your roof. Put out **rain barrels**. They will fill up with water. Use it to water your plants.

SAVE WATER AT SCHOOL

Ask if you can set up rain barrels at school. Tell your friends to set up rain barrels, too. We can all save water! What are your other ideas to help save water?

GET STARTED TODAY

- Turn the water off while you brush your teeth.

- Take shorter showers.

- Only run the dishwasher when it is full.

- Use old water from the dog dish or fish tank to water plants.

- Collect rainwater to water plants.

WORDS TO KNOW

evaporate – when water turns to a vapor or gas

rain barrel – a big bucket that catches rainwater falling off a roof

rainwater – water that falls as rain

water cycle – the way water moves around Earth

LEARN MORE

Books

Green, Jen. *Saving Water*. New York: Windmill Books, 2012.

Hawes, Alison. *Water Wise*! New York: Crabtree Publishing, 2011.

Web Sites

EPA Water Sense: Kids
http://www.epa.gov/watersense/kids/index.html
Learn simple ways to save water and why it is important.

National Geographic Kids: Water Whiz
http://kids.nationalgeographic.com/kids/games/puzzlesquizzes/water-wiz/
Find out how much water most homes in America use.

Water Use It Wisely: Kids
http://wateruseitwisely.com/kids/index.php
Play games and learn new ways to save water.

INDEX

dishwasher, 15

hose, 16

ice cubes, 15

lakes, 4, 7, 8

oceans, 4, 7

plants, 15, 18

rain, 6, 7, 18, 21
rain barrels, 18, 21
rivers, 4, 7, 8

showers, 12

trash, 8

water cycle, 6, 7